A LIFEBUILDER

MEETING THE SPIRIT

12 Studies
for individuals or groups

Douglas Connelly

With Notes for Leaders

SCRIPTURE UNION
130 City Road, London EC1V 2NJ

First published in the United States by InterVarsity Press.
First published in Great Britain by Scripture Union, 1993.

Cover photograph: Gary Irving

ISBN 0 86201 895 1

Printed in England by Ebenezer Baylis & Son Limited, The Trinity Press, Worcester and London

Contents

Getting the Most
from LifeBuilder Bible Studies

Many of us long to fill our minds and our lives with Scripture. We desire to be transformed by its message. LifeBuilder Bible Studies are designed to be an exciting and challenging way to do just that. They help us to be guided by God's Word in every area of life.

How They Work

LifeBuilders have a number of distinctive features. Perhaps the most important is that they are *inductive* rather than *deductive*. In other words, they lead us to *discover* what the Bible says rather than simply *telling* us what it says.

They are also thought-provoking. They help us to think about the meaning of the passage so that we can truly understand what the author is saying. The questions require more than one-word answers.

The studies are personal. Questions expose us to the promises, assurances, exhortations and challenges of God's Word. They are designed to allow the Scriptures to renew our minds so that we can be transformed by the Spirit of God. This is the ultimate goal of all Bible study.

The studies are versatile. They are designed for student, neighborhood and church groups. They are also effective for individual study.

How They're Put Together

LifeBuilders also have a distinctive format. Each study need take no more than forty-five minutes in a group setting or thirty minutes in personal study – unless you choose to take more time.

The studies can be used within a quarter system in a church and fit well in a semester or trimester system on a college campus. If a guide has more than thirteen studies, it is divided into two or occasionally three parts of approximately twelve studies each.

LifeBuilders use a workbook format. Space is provided for writing answers to each question. This is ideal for personal study and allows group members to prepare in advance for the discussion.

The studies also contain leader's notes. They show how to lead a group discussion, provide additional background information on certain questions, give helpful tips on group dynamics and suggest ways to deal with problems which may arise during the discussion. With such helps, someone with little or no experience can lead an effective study.

Suggestions for Individual Study

1. As you begin each study, pray that God will help you to understand and apply the passage to your life.

2. Read and reread the assigned Bible passage to familiarize yourself with what the author is saying. In the case of book studies, you may want to read through the entire book prior to the first study. This will give you a helpful overview of its contents.

3. A good modern translation of the Bible, rather than the King James Version or a paraphrase, will give you the most help. The New International Version, the New American Standard Bible and the Revised Standard Version are all recommended. However, the questions in this guide are based on the New International Version.

4. Write your answers in the space provided in the study guide. This will help you to express your understanding of the passage clearly.

5. It might be good to have a Bible dictionary handy. Use it to look up any unfamiliar words, names or places.

Suggestions for Group Study

1. Come to the study prepared. Follow the suggestions for individual study mentioned above. You will find that careful preparation will greatly enrich your time spent in group discussion.

2. Be willing to participate in the discussion. The leader of your group will not be lecturing. Instead, he or she will be encouraging the members of the group to discuss what they have learned from the passage. The leader will be asking the questions that are found in this guide. Plan to share what God has taught you in your individual study.

3. Stick to the passage being studied. Your answers should be based on the verses which are the focus of the discussion and not on outside authorities such as commentaries or speakers. This guide deliberately avoids jumping from book to book or passage to passage. Each study focuses on only one

passage. Book studies are generally designed to lead you through the book in the order in which it was written. This will help you follow the author's argument.

4. Be sensitive to the other members of the group. Listen attentively when they share what they have learned. You may be surprised by their insights! Link what you say to the comments of others so the group stays on the topic. Also, be affirming whenever you can. This will encourage some of the more hesitant members of the group to participate.

5. Be careful not to dominate the discussion. We are sometimes so eager to share what we have learned that we leave too little opportunity for others to respond. By all means participate! But allow others to also.

6. Expect God to teach you through the passage being discussed and through the other members of the group. Pray that you will have an enjoyable and profitable time together.

7. If you are the discussion leader, you will find additional suggestions and helpful ideas for each study in the leader's notes. These are found at the back of the guide.

Introducing Meeting the Spirit

I'm afraid that many followers of Jesus Christ know about as much concerning the Holy Spirit as some disciples who were asked by the apostle Paul, "Did you receive the Holy Spirit when you believed?" They responded, "No, we have not even heard that there is a Holy Spirit!"

These particular disciples were followers of John the Baptist, and I'm sure they had heard John preach about the Holy Spirit. But they had never realized that the Spirit promised by God was now available to them. They had never heard that the Holy Spirit could make a difference in their lives. Christians today have certainly heard about the Holy Spirit, but many of us have never encountered the Spirit in a life-changing way.

That is what this study guide is intended to do in your life—change it! We will examine key passages of Scripture that teach us vital truths about who the Spirit of God is and what he is anxious to do in our lives. But the goal is not simply to gain more knowledge. Our goal is to translate that knowledge into a deeper relationship with another person—a divine person—the Spirit of God. You are embarking on an exciting journey. Be prepared to emerge as a transformed person.

Three basic biblical facts will underlie everything we discuss together about the Spirit of God. The first fact is that the Spirit *is*. He exists. Belief in the Holy Spirit is not based on myth or on a religious fairy tale. As we will see, Jesus referred to the Spirit repeatedly. Every New Testament writer and many Old Testament writers refer to the Spirit of God.

The second basic fact about the Spirit is that he is a person. Christians (following the biblical example) refer to the Spirit as "he," not as "it." *Spirit* is not simply a term for God's energy or power. The Spirit is a personal being.

Because he is a person, we can relate to the Spirit in a personal way. In fact, he wants us to know him on a deeply intimate level.

The Bible is also clear in its declaration that the Spirit is a divine person. He is God. Since the first century, Christians have consistently recognized the Spirit as a member of the Trinity—God the Father, God the Son, and God the Holy Spirit. The Spirit's deity will be confirmed repeatedly as we explore the Scripture passages in this study guide.

The fact that the Spirit is God opens up all kinds of wonderful possibilities for us. As we come to develop a personal relationship with the Spirit, we are developing a relationship with God himself. Most of us already relate with Jesus, and we know how to interact with God the Father. Now we will see what it means to walk in the realm of the Spirit. I am convinced from my own study of the Spirit that our lives will be transformed beyond recognition as we appropriate and draw upon the resources we have in the Holy Spirit.

The Spirit of God already knows us completely. We have the opportunity through these studies to grow in our knowledge of the Spirit.

1
Meet the Holy Spirit!
John 16:5-15

I find it awkward to meet new people. I don't always know what to say or how to relate. It's always easier to meet someone if we are introduced to each other by a mutual friend. The person who knows us both can help us overcome those difficult initial hurdles. In this passage we are introduced to the Holy Spirit by our mutual friend, Jesus. Jesus knows us both and stands between us to help us begin to build a new relationship.

1. What impressions come to your mind when you think about the Holy Spirit?

2. John 13—17 contains Jesus' final instructions to his disciples. Read John 16:5-15. Describe the mood of the disciples as Jesus was speaking to them.

3. Why in this setting does Jesus refer to the Spirit as "the Counselor"?

4. In what ways was it to the disciples' advantage that Jesus would go away and the Spirit of God would come?

Jesus presence no longer limited
GO AWAY = Atonement

---

5. In verses 8-11 Jesus outlines the ministry of the Spirit to the world. According to these verses, what specific conviction does the Spirit bring to those who hear the message of Christ? *The aim of HS is not to produce a guilty verdict but to bring the defendant to see the perilous condition he is in" D.Carson*
Righteousness = False understanding of righteousness [*Believe 1:11, 3:19*]
cf 1 THESS 1:8

6. The "prince of this world" mentioned in verse 11 is Satan. Why is it important for the Spirit to convince the world that their "prince" is already condemned?

see 12:31 - Cross is the place where the world + its prince are condemned + defeated.

CROSS = Decisive moment of Judgement

---

7. Based on verses 12 and 13, how would you describe the Spirit's ministry to Jesus' followers? *cf 14:26*

Assurance that be led into a true understanding of the saving events about to occur.
Remind - what Jesus said + did
Reveal - significance of what Jesus said + did

---

8. The disciples listening to Jesus would later record the message of Christ in the books and letters of the New Testament. What authority does Jesus' statement impart to those writings?

Bearers of God's Word

---

9. What insight can you gain from verses 14 and 15 about the Spirit's relationship to Jesus and to the Father?

Counsellor = Son = Father

10. What significant things have you learned about the Spirit from this initial encounter?

---

11. What expectations about the Spirit would the disciples have had after listening to Jesus?

---

12. What are your expectations as you pursue a deeper relationship with the Spirit?

2
The Spirit Invades
Acts 2

When God is about to do something new, he has a powerful way of announcing it. In the Old Testament God rescued his people from Egypt with a mighty outpouring of his power. When Jesus, God's own Son, was condemned and executed, God brought him back to life in an unparalleled act of power. When God was prepared to push a few reluctant disciples on the path of world evangelization, he swept over them in another work of power. God sent the Holy Spirit. The Spirit came in a new way. The Spirit came with a new mission. Believers were thrust out with a new message. A new day had dawned!

1. Have you ever been in a worship service or prayer group and sensed the Spirit moving in a powerful way? Describe that experience and its results in your life.

2. Read Acts 2:1-13. Explain how you would have felt if you had been one of Jesus' followers and had witnessed the events of verses 1-4.

3. What was the reaction of the crowd gathered in Jerusalem?

What led them to those conclusions?

---

4. Read Acts 2:14-41. What explanation does Peter give for the strange events that were occurring?

---

5. Why do you think it was important for Peter to ground this event in the prophetic Scriptures of the Old Testament? (He quotes from Joel 2:28-32.)

---

6. The crowd already knew about Jesus' ministry, miracles and death. What was new in Peter's message (vv. 22-36)?

---

7. What does Peter promise to those who repent and believe on Jesus (v. 38)?

---

8. Think back to the last time you witnessed to a non-Christian. Which elements of Peter's sermon did you include in your presentation?

Which elements were missing?

9. Can we expect this kind of response to the gospel today, or was this a unique event for one place and time? Explain.

10. Read Acts 2:42-47. What can you discover in these verses about the activities and attitudes of these early Christians?

11. Which of these factors are missing in your church or Christian fellowship group?

12. What specific steps can you take to restore some of these basic elements of Christian faith and ministry to your church or small group?

3
The Spirit Speaks

1 Corinthians 2:1-16

The fifth inning of a televised baseball game is a great time for a nap! One recent Sunday afternoon I had drifted blissfully off to sleep when a series of loud beeps from the television brought me fully awake. The beeps were followed by these words: "We interrupt this program to bring you a severe weather bulletin." By now I was sitting up, listening intently to the message that followed. My wife, who had been in another room, was standing in the doorway totally focused on the announcement from our regional weather center. The words were intensely practical, and they came into our home with authority.

The Spirit of God speaks with the highest authority—the authority of God himself. But far too often we are content to sleep our way through it. This study will help us hear God's message with renewed intensity.

1. When have you been in a situation where you wished God would speak directly to you? Explain why you felt that way.

2. Read 1 Corinthians 2:1-16. Describe the *content* of Paul's message to the Corinthians.

Describe the spirit of Paul as God's messenger.

---

3. Paul thought it was important that his message came to the Corinthians in "the Spirit's power." What would have been the result if Paul had preached only with "wise and persuasive words" (vv. 1-5)?

How can you be confident that you have believed the true message from God and are not simply following a persuasive leader?

---

4. Why do you think most prominent people in our day (and in Paul's day) reject the message of Christ?

---

5. According to verses 9-10, what methods fail to uncover the good things that God has prepared for us?

If these methods have failed, how *can* we discover these good things from God?

---

6. Why would Paul's argument in verses 11 and 12 convince you that the Holy Spirit is God?

7. Since Paul and the other apostles are no longer here to speak to us directly, where can we find these "words taught by the Spirit" (v. 13)

---

8. What insights can you gain from verse 14 that may explain why a person may reject the message of Christ and the clear teaching of the Bible?

---

9. According to this passage what elements are required for us to have access to "the mind of Christ"?

---

10. How does your study of this passage affect how you will hear God's Word from now on?

---

11. What specific things can you ask the Holy Spirit to do in your mind and heart as you read and study the Bible?

4
The Spirit Renews
John 3:1-8

A few years ago I watched the birth of our third child. Our son Kyle emerged into the bright light of a new world. His first gasp drew air into his lungs. His next act was to let out a piercing cry. Everyone in the delivery room smiled. The cry was a sign of life.

Not long after that I witnessed the birth of a young adult woman! The birth did not take place in a hospital; it happened in a home. As she heard the message of Christ, the young woman believed. At that moment she was born into a whole new spiritual realm.

The Spirit was intimately involved in that new birth. I explained the message of the gospel. The young woman received it with faith. But the Spirit brought new life.

---

1. What thoughts and feelings do you associate with birth?

---

2. Read John 3:1-8. What kind of man do you think Nicodemus was?

---

3. How would you summarize his view of who Jesus was (v. 2)?

4. Explain Nicodemus's initial view of being "born again" (v. 4).

5. Jesus talks about two births—the first is a birth of the flesh, the second a birth of the spirit. Describe each birth in your own words.

6. What role does the Holy Spirit play in the new birth?

7. In what ways is the Spirit's work of bringing people to new birth like the blowing of the wind (v. 8)?

8. How will that understanding of the Spirit's work affect your approach to witnessing to others about Christ?

9. Have you experienced the new birth Jesus talks about in this passage? Describe how the Spirit worked in your life to bring you to Christ.

10. There are obvious signs that a person has physical life. What are the signs that a person has the spiritual life Jesus has described in this passage?

11. Which of these signs of new life is most obvious in your life?

Which is least obvious?

Thank God for the areas in which he has strengthened you, and ask him to help you grow in your areas of weakness.

5
The Spirit Empowers

Acts 6:1-15

The small man was almost hidden by the oak pulpit. His voice was soft. When he began to speak, very few in the audience listened with much interest. Within five minutes, however, every eye was riveted on the speaker. Everyone strained to hear his words. The man had spent years languishing in the prison camps of communist China for one crime—faith in Jesus Christ.

After Harry Lee spoke, I asked him one question, "How did you survive such abuse and pain?" His answer was immediate, "Whatever I needed for each hour and each crisis, the Holy Spirit provided. Never any excess. Never any lack."

1. Have you ever felt a special power come over you as you faced a physical emergency or an emotional challenge? Describe that experience.

2. Read Acts 6:1-7. Based on the information in these verses, how would you describe Stephen?

3. The Holy Spirit will empower Stephen to stand against some incredible opposition in the verses that follow. What qualities did Stephen cultivate in his life and character to prepare the way for the Spirit's work?

4. Read Acts 6:8-15. What was the core of the argument between Stephen and the Jews of the Synagogue of Freedmen?

5. How did the Spirit help Stephen stand against this opposition?

6. In what situations might you ask the Spirit for the same help?

7. Based on Stephen's experience in verses 11-14, what should you be prepared to face when you speak with the Spirit's power?

8. In your opinion, what captivated the interest of the men of the Sanhedrin as they listened to Stephen (v. 15)?

9. Read Acts 7:54-60. The outcome of Stephen's arrest was his execution! In what ways did the Spirit empower Stephen to face such a cruel death?

10. If you had to choose between being Stephen or one of those who stoned him, which would you choose and why?

11. What do you think would have been the response to this situation of a person who did not possess the Holy Spirit?

_____

12. What words or phrases would you use to describe your spiritual life?

What would be different if you were "full of faith and of the Holy Spirit"?

6
The Spirit Comforts
John 14:15-27

A crisis often reveals who our true friends are. When we've failed or fallen, most people find it convenient to avoid us. Some who claimed to be our friends abandon us. But a few prove themselves to be genuine friends by coming along beside us and helping us out of despair.

One of the Spirit's ministries is to comfort and counsel us when we are afraid or afflicted or abandoned. In this passage Jesus speaks to his troubled disciples about the Spirit's comforting power.

1. Think of a person who has helped you in a time of personal crisis or need. What did that person do to bring comfort to you?

2. Read John 14:15-27. Why were Jesus' disciples troubled?

3. What does this passage tell you about what kind of person the Spirit is?

4. What does the title "Counselor" convey to you about the Spirit's ministry?

5. Jesus said that the Spirit who had been "with" the disciples would soon live "in" the disciples (v. 17). Why is that change significant?

6. Contrast the Spirit's relationship to those who are not Jesus' followers ("the world," v. 17) with the Spirit's relationship to those who are Jesus' followers (vv. 17-19).

7. What comes to mind when you think of being abandoned as an "orphan"?

8. How will the Holy Spirit bring comfort to these followers of Jesus (vv. 26-27)?

9. In what ways has the Spirit helped or comforted you?

10. How does Christ's peace differ from the peace the world offers?

11. On a scale from 1 (absolute calm) to 10 (extreme unrest), what is your level of peace right now? Why?

---

12. What specific steps can you take in a time of personal crisis to gain access to the Spirit's comfort and counsel?

7
The Spirit Guides
Acts 16:1-15

Ilf I just knew what God wanted me to do."

This statement often comes to our minds and lips as we face difficult decisions. Probably no aspect of the Christian life is more frustrating than discovering the will of God.

Two factors contribute to our frustration. First, we usually want God to give us answers when what he promises to give us is wisdom. Second, we are not aware of the Spirit's work of guiding us through times of uncertainty. Because we don't know that the Spirit is willing and anxious to work in such a way, we don't anticipate his ministry in our lives. As a result, we don't sense the Spirit's leading.

In this passage from the book of Acts, Paul and his companions experience the Spirit's guidance in a powerful way.

1. Think back to a time when you needed the Lord's direction in a decision. How did you seek out God's will?

2. Read Acts 16:1-10. What factors in verses 1-5 demonstrate that Paul was acting in obedience to the Lord?

3. Paul and his companions first experienced the negative leading of the Spirit. They were not allowed to enter certain regions or to preach in some areas (vv. 6-7). How do you think the Spirit told Paul not to proceed into these places?

4. Some Christians believe that Paul made a mistake by even trying to enter these regions. They think he should have waited for clear direction from God before taking any initiative. Explain why you agree or disagree with that view.

5. Positive direction from the Spirit came by means of a vision to Paul. What was it about the vision and Paul's circumstances that would lead Paul to conclude "God had called us to preach the gospel" in the new region of Macedonia (v. 10)?

6. What principles can you draw from Paul's experience that will help you know when the Spirit is directing you?

7. In what practical ways can you test what you (or what someone else) believe is the Lord's direction in a decision?

8. Read Acts 16:11-15. What facts in these verses confirm that Paul's earlier vision was indeed from the Lord?

9. Should we look for confirming evidence of the Spirit's leading in our lives? (For example, can we determine the Spirit's leading simply by results? If a decision brings difficulty or inconvenience with it, does that mean it was not God's will?) Explain your answer.

10. When you are faced with a decision, what steps will you follow as you seek the Spirit's direction?

What specific things will you expect to receive from the Spirit as you seek his leading?

11. What practical counsel and help can you offer to another believer who is struggling with discerning the will of God?

8
The Spirit Liberates
Romans 8:1-27

W e live in a society that claims to be free. In reality, the people in our society are often enslaved. The cry of men and women today is to be free to do what they want, when they want, where they want—and they call it "freedom." The Bible calls it "slavery."

Genuine freedom comes when we enslave ourselves to God. We are set free from the old masters of sin and death. We serve our new Master with joyful obedience.

The source of real liberation is the Spirit of God. He liberates the human spirit from the bondage of sin. In Romans 8 the apostle Paul reaches the height of adoration and praise to the life-giving and liberating Spirit.

1. What images come to your mind when you think of liberation or freedom?

2. Read Romans 8:1-27. What was it like for Paul when he lived under the old taskmasters of the law, sin and death?

3. How did God set us free from the condemnation of the law (v. 3)?

He sends his Son to do what the law was powerless
to do — Justify + sanctify — Incarnation + Atonement
i) Sent his Son ii) " " the likeness of sinful man
iii) To be a sin offering iv) condemned sin in sinful man
iv) In order that the righteous requirements will be met in us

4. How does God set us free from being dominated by our sinful nature (vv. 4-9)?

Gives us the Holy Spirit so that we can set our minds on the what the Spirit desires, submit to God's law + please God.

5. How does God set us free from the destruction of death (vv. 10-11)?

He gives us his Spirit to give our Spirits life. Spirit will give our bodies life

6. If we are no longer under obligation to these old masters, why do we choose so often to submit again to their authority?

How can we be more effective in resisting them?

7. List the specific ministries of the Spirit described in verses 12-17.

i) Victory over sin ii) Guidance iii) Adoption iv) Certainty

8. One aspect of the Spirit's ministry is to give us confidence before the Father. In what ways does the truth explained in verses 15-17 help you to relate more positively to the Father?

9. What does it mean to you that you are not God's slave but his child (v. 16)?

10. Even those of us who have the Spirit of God find ourselves "groaning inwardly" at times as we wait for our full redemption. Is that true in your experience? Explain your answer with specific examples.

_____

11. In what ways does the Spirit minister to us in our weakness (vv. 26-27)?

_____

12. Which of the Spirit's ministries described in this chapter encourages you most at this point in your life?

How will you live differently as a result of your knowledge of that ministry of the Spirit of God to you?

9
The Spirit Equips
1 Corinthians 12

When I talked to Bill about being part of our ushering team, his response was "That's not my gift." Since he had responded the same way for several other positions in ministry, I said, "What exactly *is* your gift?"

"I'm not sure," he shot back. "I think it's just to be an observer."

I knew from Bill's answer that he wasn't concerned about using "his gift" at all. He didn't want any responsibility.

The subject of spiritual gifts has created tremendous debate among Christians. In some circles an emphasis on gifts is all you will hear about. In other fellowships the subject is totally avoided. The New Testament, however, presents a very balanced perspective.

Spiritual gifts are not all there is to the Christian life. But the Christian life cannot be lived effectively without using these marvelous grace gifts from God's Spirit.

---

1. What issues come to your mind when you think about spiritual gifts?

---

2. Read 1 Corinthians 12:1-31. What does this passage tell you about how gifts and the Spirit work together?

What does it tell you about how gifts and the body work together?

3. Paul lists several spiritual gifts in verses 8-10. Briefly describe each one.

4. Give an example of how you have seen one of these gifts demonstrated.

5. Why is it so important for Paul to talk about the unity of Christ's body at the same time that he talks about spiritual gifts (vv. 12-20)?

6. In your opinion are spiritual gifts different from natural abilities? Explain your answer.

7. The Spirit links believers in Christ together. In what practical ways should this truth affect the composition of your church or fellowship group?

How should it change the way you relate to each person in it?

8. Why does Paul emphasize that it is God who has placed the members of the body together as he desires?

_____

9. According to this passage, what specific responsibilities do you have toward other members of the body?

_____

10. What would you say that your spiritual gift or gifts are?

_____

11. How are you using your gifts to build up Christ's body?

10
The Spirit Transforms
Galatians 5:13-26

The television evangelist was captivating in his delivery. The crowd of people seated before him hung on every word. He quoted from the Bible with ease. What made me turn off the program was not his message or his style. It was his arrogance.

Some Christians are highly gifted and use their gifts to touch a wide audience. As they focus on their gifts, however, they can easily forget the fruit of the Spirit. The presence of the Holy Spirit in our lives does not display itself in what we do as much as in who we are. The evidence of the Spirit's presence is a changed character.

1. How does it affect you when someone approaches you with an unloving or negative spirit?

2. Read Galatians 5:13-26. We, as Christians, have been set free in Christ. According to these verses, what are some of the limitations on that freedom?

3. Describe a recent example of the conflict between the sinful nature and the Spirit in your life.

4. Which of the expressions of the sinful nature outlined in verses 19-21 do you find most apparent in our society?

In what ways is it displayed?

5. What do you think Paul means when he says in verse 21, "Those who live like this will not inherit the kingdom of God"?

6. Why does Paul refer to the qualities in verses 22-26 as the "fruit" of the Spirit?

7. Describe each aspect of the fruit of the Spirit and explain how that quality is demonstrated in a person's life.

8. If we have crucified the sinful nature with its passions and desires as verse 24 says, then why do we still struggle with its power?

9. In the context of the passage, what does it mean to "keep in step with the Spirit" (v. 25)?

10. As you look over the list of qualities that demonstrate the Spirit's presence in a person's life, which of them is most lacking in your life?

What specific steps can you take to cultivate that quality?

11
The Spirit Influences
Ephesians 5:15-21

N one of us wants to be controlled by someone else. Particularly in the realm of our spiritual life, we cringe at the thought of someone being in control of our lives. Even the word *control* makes us think of the mindless obedience demanded by certain cults. Their members seem to give up their wills, and even rational thought, in false reverence for a human leader.

As Christians, however, we are called to be controlled—not by a human leader or by the dictates of a cult, but by the Spirit of God. When we are filled by the Spirit, we will live like the Lord Jesus.

---

1. Have you ever had another Christian try to dictate how you should live? What was (or would be) your response to that person?

---

2. Read Ephesians 5:15-21. Based on Paul's exhortation in verses 15 and 16, describe Paul's view of the society and times in which we live.

Do you agree with his evaluation? Why or why not?

3. What does verse 17 tell you about the importance of the instruction that follows?

---

4. How can the command regarding wine in verse 18 be applied to other practices or areas of life?

---

5. How does the analogy of being "drunk with wine" (or, "under the influence of alcohol") help you understand what it means to be "filled with the Spirit"?

---

6. What is the difference between being controlled by a human spiritual leader and being controlled by the Holy Spirit?

---

7. How will a person who is filled with the Spirit act?

---

8. According to these verses, what is required of a person in order to be filled with the Spirit?

---

9. What will characterize your relationship with the Lord when you are filled with the Spirit?

10. Verse 21 tells us that we should submit to one another. How does this command relate to the verses that precede it?

---

11. Describe someone you know or have read about (in the Bible or elsewhere) whom you would consider to be filled with the Spirit.

---

12. How can you tell whether you are filled with the Spirit in your own life?

12
The Spirit Unifies
Ephesians 4:1-16

Ⅰf Jesus wanted his followers to be one, why are there so many denominations and divisions in the church?"

This question has plagued the minds of Christians for centuries. As we will see in this study, Christ did want his followers to be bound together in unity. That unity, however, is not displayed in organizational oneness. It focuses instead on Christ as the Head and the Spirit as the divine Unifier. Unfortunately, even that level of unity is not demonstrated very often among Christians.

As we examine this passage, we will learn how we can share in the Spirit's work of bringing maturity and unity to Christ's body. As we contribute our gifts to build up others, we in turn are built up ourselves.

1. Why do you think there is such division among Christian churches?

2. Read Ephesians 4:1-16. What words and phrases does Paul use in this passage to emphasize the importance of unity among Christ's followers?

3. In what ways do the qualities listed in verse 2 contribute to a spirit of unity?

4. Which of these qualities do you find most difficult to demonstrate in your life?

5. Why does preserving the unity of the Spirit require such diligent effort (v. 3)?

6. In verses 4-6 Paul lists seven points of unity among believers in Christ. What are they, and why is each important?

7. In his grace Christ has given gifted leaders to the church as apostles, prophets, evangelists, pastors and teachers. If you visualize the church as a human body, what parts of the body are each of these leaders? (Remember that Christ is the head.)

8. Using the picture of the human body again, what parts of the body would you most like to be and why?

How are your spiritual gifts (see question 10 in study 9) related to the functions of the part you selected?

9. What are the goals behind each Christian's works of ministry in the body of Christ (vv. 12-13)?

10. What are the results if believers fail to build each other up in the faith (v. 14)?

11. Why will "speaking the truth in love" help the body grow to maturity?

12. How would you summarize the Spirit's role in producing and preserving unity in the body of Christ?

13. What specific steps can you take to restore or strengthen spiritual unity to your circle of Christian fellowship?

Leader's Notes

Leading a Bible discussion can be an enjoyable and rewarding experience. But it can also be *scary*—especially if you've never done it before. If this is your feeling, you're in good company. When God asked Moses to lead the Israelites out of Egypt, he replied, "O Lord, please send someone else to do it!" (Ex 4:13).

When Solomon became king of Israel, he felt the task was beyond his abilities. "I am only a little child and do not know how to carry out my duties. . . . Who is able to govern this great people of yours?" (1 Kings 3:7, 9).

When God called Jeremiah to be a prophet, he replied, "Ah, Sovereign LORD, . . . I do not know how to speak; I am only a child" (Jer 1:6).

The list goes on. The apostles were "unschooled, ordinary men" (Acts 4:13). Timothy was young, frail and frightened. Paul's "thorn in the flesh" made him feel weak. But God's response to all of his servants—including you—is essentially the same: "My grace is sufficient for you" (2 Cor 12:9). Relax. God helped these people in spite of their weaknesses, and he can help you in spite of your feelings of inadequacy.

There is another reason why you should feel encouraged. Leading a Bible discussion is not difficult if you follow certain guidelines. You don't need to be an expert on the Bible or a trained teacher. The suggestions listed below should enable you to effectively and enjoyably fulfill your role as leader.

Preparing to Lead

1. Ask God to help you understand and apply the passage to your own life. Unless this happens, you will not be prepared to lead others. Pray too for the various members of the group. Ask God to give you an enjoyable and profitable time together studying his Word.

2. As you begin each study, read and reread the assigned Bible passage to familiarize yourself with what the author is saying. In the case of book studies, you may want to read through the entire book prior to the first study. This will give you a helpful overview of its contents.

3. This study guide is based on the New International Version of the Bible. It will help you and the group if you use this translation as the basis for your study and discussion. Encourage others to use the NIV also, but allow them the freedom to use whatever translation they prefer.

4. Carefully work through each question in the study. Spend time in meditation and reflection as you formulate your answers.

5. Write your answers in the space provided in the study guide. This will help you to express your understanding of the passage clearly.

6. It might help you to have a Bible dictionary handy. Use it to look up any unfamiliar words, names or places. (For additional help on how to study a passage, see chapter five of *Leading Bible Discussions*, SU.)

7. Once you have finished your own study of the passage, familiarize yourself with the leader's notes for the study you are leading. These are designed to help you in several ways. First, they tell you the purpose the study guide author had in mind while writing the study. Take time to think through how the study questions work together to accomplish that purpose. Second, the notes provide you with additional background information or comments on some of the questions. This information can be useful if people have difficulty understanding or answering a question. Third, the leader's notes can alert you to potential problems you may encounter during the study.

8. If you wish to remind yourself of anything mentioned in the leader's notes, make a note to yourself below that question in the study.

Leading the Study

1. Begin the study on time. Unless you are leading an evangelistic Bible study, open with prayer, asking God to help you to understand and apply the passage.

2. Be sure that everyone in your group has a study guide. Encourage them to prepare beforehand for each discussion by working through the questions in the guide.

3. At the beginning of your first time together, explain that these studies are meant to be discussions not lectures. Encourage the members of the group to participate. However, do not put pressure on those who may be hesitant to speak during the first few sessions.

4. Read the introductory paragraph at the beginning of the discussion. This will orient the group to the passage being studied.

5. Read the passage aloud if you are studying one chapter or less. You may choose to do this yourself, or someone else may read if he or she has been asked to do so prior to the study. Longer passages may occasionally be read in parts at different times during the study. Some studies may cover several chapters. In such cases reading aloud would probably take too much time, so the group members should simply read the assigned passages prior to the study.

6. As you begin to ask the questions in the guide, keep several things in mind. First, the questions are designed to be used just as they are written. If you wish, you may simply read them aloud to the group. Or you may prefer to express them in your own words. However, unnecessary rewording of the questions is not recommended.

Second, the questions are intended to guide the group toward understanding and applying the *main idea* of the passage. The author of the guide has stated his or her view of this central idea in the *purpose* of the study in the leader's notes. You should try to understand how the passage expresses this idea and how the study questions work together to lead the group in that direction.

There may be times when it is appropriate to deviate from the study guide. For example, a question may have already been answered. If so, move on to the next question. Or someone may raise an important question not covered in the guide. Take time to discuss it! The important thing is to use discretion. There may be many routes you can travel to reach the goal of the study. But the easiest route is usually the one the author has suggested.

7. Avoid answering your own questions. If necessary, repeat or rephrase them until they are clearly understood. An eager group quickly becomes passive and silent if they think the leader will do most of the talking.

8. Don't be afraid of silence. People may need time to think about the question before formulating their answers.

9. Don't be content with just one answer. Ask, "What do the rest of you think?" or "Anything else?" until several people have given answers to the question.

10. Acknowledge all contributions. Try to be affirming whenever possible. Never reject an answer. If it is clearly wrong, ask, "Which verse led you to that conclusion?" or again, "What do the rest of you think?"

11. Don't expect every answer to be addressed to you, even though this will probably happen at first. As group members become more at ease, they will begin to truly interact with each other. This is one sign of a healthy discussion.

12. Don't be afraid of controversy. It can be very stimulating. If you don't resolve an issue completely, don't be frustrated. Move on and keep it in mind for later. A subsequent study may solve the problem.

13. Stick to the passage under consideration. It should be the source for answering the questions. Discourage the group from unnecessary cross-referencing. Likewise, stick to the subject and avoid going off on tangents.

14. Periodically summarize what the *group* has said about the passage. This helps to draw together the various ideas mentioned and gives continuity to the study. But don't preach.

15. Conclude your time together with conversational prayer. Be sure to ask God's help to apply those things which you learned in the study.

16. End on time.

Many more suggestions and helps are found in *Leading Bible Discussions* (SU). Reading and studying through that would be well worth your time.

Components of Small Groups

A healthy small group should do more than study the Bible. There are four components you should consider as you structure your time together.

Nurture. Being a part of a small group should be a nurturing and edifying experience. You should grow in your knowledge and love of God and each other. If we are to properly love God, we must know and keep his commandments (Jn 14:15). That is why Bible study should be a foundational part of your small group. But you can be nurtured by other things as well. You can memorize Scripture, read and discuss a book, or occasionally listen to a tape of a good speaker.

Community. Most people have a need for close friendships. Your small group can be an excellent place to cultivate such relationships. Allow time for informal interaction before and after the study. Have a time of sharing during the meeting. Do fun things together as a group, such as a potluck supper or a picnic. Have someone bring refreshments to the meeting. Be creative!

Worship. A portion of your time together can be spent in worship and prayer. Praise God together for who he is. Thank him for what he has done and is doing in your lives and in the world. Pray for each other's needs. Ask God to help you to apply what you have learned. Sing hymns together.

Mission. Many small groups decide to work together in some form of outreach. This can be a practical way of applying what you have learned. You can host a series of evangelistic discussions for your friends or neighbors. You can visit people at a home for the elderly. Help a widow with cleaning or repair jobs around her home. Such projects can have a transforming influence on your group.

For a detailed discussion of the nature and function of small groups, read

Small Group Leaders' Handbook or *Good Things Come in Small Groups* (both from SU).

Study 1. Meet the Holy Spirit! John 16:5-15.
Purpose: To introduce the student to the Holy Spirit and to the Spirit's ministry.
General Introduction: The Bible's teaching on the Holy Spirit is extensive. As the group leader, you will find it helpful to read a survey of this area of truth before the study group begins.

Be sure to choose material that will lead you into a deeper understanding of the biblical teaching on the subject, not just through the controversies of modern theologians. Any standard book on systematic theology will include a section on the Holy Spirit. Single volume studies abound, too. Three of the best are:

Charles Ryrie, *The Holy Spirit* (Chicago: Moody Press, 1965; reprinted 1992).

Michael Green, *I Believe in the Holy Spirit* (London: Hodder & Stoughton, 1985).

R.C. Sproul, *The Mystery of the Holy Spirit* (Christian Focus, 1991).

Once you have a broader view of the biblical teaching on the Holy Spirit, you will be better equipped to answer questions that may arise during group discussion.

The doctrine of the Holy Spirit is also one of the most controversial areas of Christian theology. Be prepared for some disagreements in your group! It is valuable, of course, to explore all sides of a controversial issue, but strive to come back to a biblical foundation for any conclusions.

The emphasis throughout these studies should be on the student's personal response to the truth that is discovered. A question that should be asked often as you conclude a study is: "How will you live (think, act) differently as the result of what we have learned?"

Question 1. Every study begins with an "approach" question, which is meant to be asked before the passage is read. These questions are important for several reasons.

First, they help the group to warm up to each other. No matter how well a group may know each other, there is always a stiffness that needs to be overcome before people will begin to talk openly. A good question will break the ice.

Second, approach questions get people thinking along the lines of the topic of the study. Most people will have lots of different things going on in their minds (dinner, an important meeting coming up, how to get the car fixed) that will have nothing to do with the study. A creative question will get their attention and draw them into the discussion.

Third, approach questions can reveal where our thoughts or feelings need to be transformed by Scripture. That is why it is especially important not to read the passage before the approach question is asked. The passage will tend to color the honest reactions people would otherwise give because they are, of course, supposed to think the way the Bible does. Giving honest responses before they find out what the Bible says may help them see where their thoughts or attitudes need to be changed.

Question 2. The leader should read through these chapters in John's Gospel as part of the preparation for this study. Jesus spoke about the Holy Spirit in several sections of this discourse. Look for insights into the mood of the disciples and how Jesus' words addressed their fears and concerns.

Question 3. The Greek word translated "Counselor" is *paraklētos*. (You will often hear the Spirit referred to as the "Paraclete.") The word refers to someone who is called alongside to give assistance. It is a difficult word to translate into one English word. Other versions use the words "Comforter," "Helper," "Advocate," or "Friend."

Question 4. Jesus' personal presence was limited to those immediately around him. The Spirit, on the other hand, would be accessible to every believer.

Question 5. The Spirit is at work whenever the message of Christ is proclaimed to convict or to convince those who hear of the truth of the message. The Spirit convinces those who hear that they have committed personal sin, that Jesus is the only righteous one, and that judgment will come upon those who refuse Christ's offer of salvation.

Question 8. Jesus makes it clear that the Spirit would have a special ministry to the disciples to remind them of Jesus' teaching and to lead them into the truth. Jesus placed his stamp of approval on the words of the apostles before those words were ever written as our New Testament Scriptures.

Question 9. Jesus speaks of the Counselor as an equal to himself and the Father. This is indirect testimony to the Spirit's deity. Jesus also speaks of the Spirit as a distinct person rather than simply a force or the expression of God's power.

Question 11. Emphasize the point that the disciples knew some facts about the Holy Spirit after this conversation but they only came to know the Spirit as they personally experienced the Spirit's presence and power.

Study 2. The Spirit Invades. Acts 2.

Purpose: To help us understand the Spirit's powerful coming on the Day of Pentecost and to show how that event affects our lives today.

Question 1. Personal experiences of the Spirit's moving will vary widely. Some may have seen outward evidences of the Spirit's work as people were moved to repentance or faith in Christ. Some may have seen miraculous events. Others may have been quietly moved to renewed commitment to Christ or to a new level of devotion. Allow individuals to share briefly in order to get the group thinking about the Spirit's sweeping power.

Question 2. The Feast of Pentecost was a Jewish holy day instituted in the Law of Moses. It took place fifty days after the Feast of Passover. Pentecost was also referred to as the Feast of Weeks (see Leviticus 23:15-21). The feast celebrated God's provision of a new harvest. In the days of Jesus it was also viewed as the anniversary of the giving of the Law to Moses on Mount Sinai. Jews from throughout the Roman Empire came to Jerusalem for this observance.

The events in Acts 2 took place just seven weeks after Jesus' death and resurrection and just ten days after Jesus' ascension into heaven (cf. Acts 1:3).

Question 5. The coming of the Spirit in a new way was not a surprise in God's plan. Just as the arrival of the Messiah had been predicted by the prophets, so a great outpouring of the Spirit had been declared centuries before it happened. The people of Israel should not have been surprised by what was happening. They should have been expecting the fulfillment of God's promise.

Question 6. The new message of the gospel centered around the resurrection of Jesus and his exaltation to the position of Lord. Jesus' resurrection was proof that he was the Messiah from God.

Question 7. This verse (Acts 2:38) may create discussion (and disagreement) about the relationship between water baptism and salvation. You may want to allow some expression of each position, but that issue is not the focus of this study. The question in the study guide focuses on the results of faith in Christ, not on the process involved.

Question 8. Depending on the makeup of your group, you may wish to substitute the following question: "What elements combined to produce such an overwhelming response to Peter's message?" Then, move on to question 9.

Question 10. Don't neglect to point out the attitudes of these early Christians—awe before God, praise, genuine concern for each other.

Question 11. As individuals explain what elements are missing in their church or small group, do not allow the discussion to become a gripe session. You are looking for honest evaluation but also some personal involvement in providing a solution.

Study 3. The Spirit Speaks. 1 Corinthians 2:1-16.
Purpose: To show the Spirit's involvement in the writing of the Scriptures and

to deepen our respect for the authority of the Bible.

Question 3. The Roman world was filled with philosophers and religious leaders who tried to capture the allegiance of people with powerful and persuasive arguments. In Corinth (and in nearby Athens) an appeal to human reason worked with particular effectiveness. Paul's message of a crucified Savior appeared moronic when compared to these sophisticated philosophies. Paul himself appeared weak and ineffective as a speaker. The difference was that the gospel did its work! Men and women were made new as the Spirit of God drew them to faith in Christ.

Question 5. Human observation and reason are not the right tools to use to discover truth about God. The truth that unaided human reason has failed to discover has been revealed to us by the Spirit (v. 10).

Question 7. This passage is a key text supporting the authority and truthfulness of the apostles' writings in the New Testament. These men did not write their own opinions but the Spirit's words.

Question 9. The Word of God and the Spirit of God combine to give us a great gift—the mind of Christ.

Question 11. Be sure to emphasize the importance of seeking the Spirit's enlightenment even as we study Scripture passages about the Spirit! If the Spirit was the source of the Scriptures and if God's truth can only be fully understood with the Spirit's help, we should consciously ask the Spirit to open our minds every time we approach the Bible.

Study 4. The Spirit Renews. John 3:1-8.

Purpose: To confront the student with the necessity of the new birth from the Spirit of God.

Question 2. Nicodemus was a member of the Jewish religious party called the Pharisees. He was meticulous in his observance of the Old Testament law. He was also a member of the Sanhedrin (the Jewish ruling council) and was, therefore, held in the highest regard by the religious leadership.

Question 5. Nicodemus would have placed high value on his birth in the flesh. He was a descendant of Abraham, part of God's people of Israel. Jesus makes it clear, however, that Nicodemus's first birth was not enough to bring him into God's kingdom.

Some Christians believe that, when Jesus says we must be born "of water and the Spirit," he is referring to water baptism. It seems best, however, to view Jesus' reference to water in relation to our first birth. "Water" (in our mother's womb) was the necessary accompaniment to the first birth of the flesh. The "Spirit" is the necessary accompaniment to our second birth.

Question 7. The blowing wind is a powerful symbol of the active Spirit. The wind is unseen but effective. The wind is "sovereign" (that is, not under human control). The wind is seen only in its effect on those it touches. In the same ways the Spirit works in our lives.

Question 9. Use this question as an opportunity to present the gospel if you have those in your group who have not believed on Christ. Ask for volunteers to share a positive testimony of their salvation.

Question 10. The new birth produces new life, and life gives evidence of its presence. New life in Christ produces new desires, new habits, and new behavior. Be careful to avoid legalistic answers to this question such as "Christians show they are born again by going to church every Sunday" or "Christians don't do . . ." Focus more on the believer's desire to be like Christ in every area of life.

Study 5. The Spirit Empowers. Acts 6:1-15.

Purpose: To awaken in us a new awareness of the Spirit's power and his willingness to empower us to do the will of God.

Introduction: Harry Lee's story is told in *From the Claws of the Dragon* by Carroll Hunt (Grand Rapids, Mich.: Zondervan, 1988).

Question 3. The Spirit alone decides where he will work in power. Jesus said in John 3, "The wind blows wherever it pleases." But the Spirit will also seek a prepared person through whom to work. Stephen prepared himself by humble service in the church, by diligent study of God's Word (revealed in his defense in chapter 7), and by cultivating a life of faith and obedience toward God.

Question 5. The Spirit's help is made evident by the inability of the Jews to confuse Stephen or to make him back away from the truth. His opponents, in fact, were forced to back down from the debate.

Question 7. The Sanhedrin was the same Jewish council that a few weeks earlier had condemned Jesus (Mk 14:55) and later had tried to silence Peter and John (Acts 4:5-7, 18-20). The false accusation brought against Stephen was that he was predicting the temple's destruction and the abolition of Jewish custom. Compare Matthew 26:59-66.

Study 6. The Spirit Comforts. John 14:15-27.

Purpose: To demonstrate the Spirit's concern and personal ministry to each of us.

Question 2. You may want to remind the group of the context of John 14. We learned in the first study that John 13—17 contains Jesus' final words to his disciples before his death. Two verses particularly reveal the mood of the disciples as they listened to Jesus—John 13:33 and 14:1.

Question 3. Focus on the closeness of the Spirit to us and the permanence of his ministry to those who are Christ's followers ("with you forever"). You may also want to discuss the significance of the title "the Spirit of truth" and the implications of that title for the Spirit's ministry.

Question 4. The title "Counselor" was discussed in the note to question 3 in the first study. The emphasis here should be on the Spirit's personal presence and care when we find ourselves in troubling circumstances.

Question 5. The Spirit of God had ministered to the disciples from an external vantage point, much like the Spirit's ministry throughout the Old Testament. But in the future (beginning most likely on the Day of Pentecost in Acts 2), the Spirit would indwell believers. Temporary empowerment of a few was replaced by a permanent indwelling of all. This indwelling also opened the way for a more intimate relationship with the Spirit than the disciples had known before.

Study 7. The Spirit Guides. Acts 16:1-15.

Purpose: To help us rely more on the Holy Spirit as we seek to know and follow God's will for our lives.

General Note: Christians do struggle with this issue of knowing the will of God. Much of the problem comes because we tend to view God's will as a tiny spot ("the center of God's will") or as a tightrope from which we can easily fall. It has helped me to see God's will as a path. Sometimes the path is wide and many options may all be included in God's will. At other times the path is quite narrow as God leads us in a very specific direction. The keys are to seek to please God in the decisions we make and to obey his Word. As we do that, we can also be confident of God's leading.

You may want to read or recommend Garry Friesen's book *Decision Making and the Will of God* (Portland, Ore.: Multnomah Press, 1981). It gives a balanced, liberating perspective on the will of God.

In this passage in Acts, the Spirit of God leads Paul and his companions down a fairly narrow path toward a precise objective—the proclamation of the gospel in Greece. It will help your group to understand the context of the passage if you use a map to show them Paul's route through Asia Minor and into Macedonia. Any Bible dictionary or handbook will outline this section of Paul's second evangelistic journey. A large map or small handout map will keep everyone together as you work through the various stages of Paul's journey.

Question 1. As individuals share their personal experiences in seeking God's will, you may want to ask them if they were confident that God was leading them at the time of the decision and what factors about the decision gave them that confidence.

Question 2. It is important to note here that negative direction from the Holy Spirit does not indicate God's disapproval or chastening. We may be walking in obedience to God and still encounter closed doors and barricades.

Paul was fulfilling God's call to preach the gospel. Christians were strengthened by his ministry. But still God would close some doors in order to point Paul to a greater opportunity.

Question 3. This is largely a speculation question but it will give members of your group the opportunity to express their opinions on how God told Paul not to enter these regions.

Question 9. The Lord's direction to Paul was confirmed by the opening of people's hearts to the gospel. But what if no one in Macedonia had believed his message? Could he have concluded that God had not called him there?

You may need to caution the members of your group about always looking for some external confirmation of God's leading. Sometimes God may lead us into difficult circumstances. At those times all we may have is the internal confirmation of the Spirit.

Study 8. The Spirit Liberates. Romans 8:1-27.

Purpose: To prepare us to understand and to act upon our liberty in Christ from the domination of sin and our old nature.

Question 3. The law of God was not evil. It was holy and good (see Romans 7:7, 12). The problem was in our sinful nature. Whoever tried to keep God's law failed. God sent his own Son to remove the burden of the law from us by offering himself as an eternal sacrifice for our sin.

Question 4. In verses 4-9 Paul contrasts the person who has never believed on Christ ("those who live according to the sinful nature") with the person who has believed ("those who live in accordance with the Spirit"). The drag of the sinful nature on our minds and behavior is counteracted by the indwelling Spirit of God.

Verse 9 also settles the issue of the relationship of salvation and the indwelling of the Spirit. Any person who is in Christ by faith is also indwelt by the Spirit.

Question 5. The destruction of death is overcome in two stages according to these verses. First we were dead in our spirit toward God but now our spirit has been made alive. Secondly, the death of our body will be overcome by our future resurrection. In both stages the Spirit is actively involved.

Question 6. The old way of life still has a powerful attraction to it. Our flesh prods us to return to the old sinful ways. As we cultivate a lifestyle in the realm of the Spirit, however, we become more and more accustomed to a life of godliness.

Question 11. One of the most comforting ministries of the Spirit is that he intercedes for us with the Father when we don't know how to pray. You may want to tie this to the intercessory ministry of Jesus (see Hebrews 7:25).

Study 9. The Spirit Equips. 1 Corinthians 12.

Purpose: To challenge us to discover and to use our spiritual gifts.

Question 1. This study will likely be the most controversial in the series. The leader needs to be on guard against two potential problems that often surface in discussions about spiritual gifts.

The first potential problem is that someone will use the discussion as a platform to champion a certain position on spiritual gifts. This seems to arise most often in regard to the sign gifts such as speaking in tongues, miraculous healing, etc. If differing viewpoints are represented in your group, give each position the opportunity to speak but do not allow one person (or position) to dominate. The issue of spiritual gifts is much broader than simply whether or not the miraculous gifts are functioning today.

The second potential problem arises when a person uses ridicule to attack a position with which that person disagrees. Any discussion of spiritual truth should be marked by kindness and respect. Otherwise the very Person we are discussing, the Holy Spirit, is grieved and his power is quenched.

Question 2. Spiritual gifts are distributed by the Spirit to every believer. It is clear that no one is left out. But the gifts are given to be used in building up the body of Christ. No one is gifted for himself or herself alone. The leader should emphasize the purpose of the gifts throughout the discussion. Gifts are given to be used in a practical, purposeful way to encourage other believers.

Question 3. For a detailed explanation of each of these gifts, you may want to consult: Leslie Flynn, *Nineteen Gifts of the Spirit* (Wheaton: Victor Books, 1975); Donald Bridge and David Phypers, *Spiritual Gifts and the Church* (Downers Grove: InterVarsity Press, 1974); Michael Green's excellent chapter on spiritual gifts (chapter 10) in his book *I Believe in the Holy Spirit*. Those desiring an in-depth study may want to use another LifeBuilder Bible Study, *Spiritual Gifts* by Charles and Anne Hummel.

Question 5. The proper use of spiritual gifts should contribute to the harmonious functioning of the body. Far too often, however, the issue of spiritual gifts brings division and bitter dispute.

Question 6. This question will produce several opinions from the group. Spiritual gifts are given by the Spirit, but the Spirit can also enhance natural ability (for example, vocal talent) to produce spiritual results.

Question 8. Spiritual gifts or their results are never to be used as a measure for comparison between believers. We are gifted by God and used in the body as he desires. The size of our ministry is irrelevant.

Question 10. Some in your group may not be able to answer this question. They can be helped to discover their gifts in two ways. First, they can work through some resource material on spiritual gifts that will help them evaluate their lives and possible gifts. Some helpful tools are listed above under question 3.

Another way to discover our spiritual gifts is to become involved in various ministries as God gives us the opportunity. It is often in the process of ministry that we discover what our gifts are. The evaluation of others in the body of Christ will also help us see areas where we are most effective in ministry. You may want to take the time to go around the group and affirm the strengths and gifts you see in each other.

Study 10. The Spirit Transforms. Galatians 5:13-26.

Purpose: To give us practical help in cultivating the fruit of the Spirit in our lives.

Question 2. Our liberty in Christ is never to be used as a cloak for sinful or selfish behavior. Our liberty is limited by our obedience to Christ as Lord and by the needs of our brothers and sisters in Christ.

Question 3. The New International Version uses the phrase *sinful nature* to translate the Greek word normally translated "the flesh." The New Testament makes it clear that when we believe in Christ our old nature is crucified with Christ (Gal 2:20; Col 3:3), and we are made a new creation, that is, we receive a new nature (2 Cor 5:17). But, in our human bodies, the desire for sin still resides (Rom 7:21-23). That sinful impulse is called *the flesh.*

I have used the phrase *sinful nature* when the text of the NIV uses it simply to avoid confusion. The struggle in the Christian, however, is not between the old nature and the new nature. The struggle is between the flesh, dragging us toward the old sinful way of life, and the Spirit, encouraging us to a new way of life.

Question 4. Do not allow the discussion on this question to go too far. The emphasis of the study is on the dramatic difference in character and behavior between those controlled by the sinful nature and those controlled by the Spirit of God.

Question 5. Paul does not mean that Christians are incapable of these acts nor that we cease to be Christians if we commit an act that comes from the sinful flesh within us. His point is that people who live a life marked by these things give evidence by that very lifestyle that they are not members of God's kingdom.

Question 6. If you walk into an orchard you can quickly discover what kind of trees are there by looking at the fruit which they produce. You discover the true nature of a person by observing the "fruit" produced in his or her life. A person who claims to be in Christ and indwelt by the Spirit will produce evidence of that claim by displaying godly character.

Question 7. Paul deliberately uses the singular ("fruit" rather than "fruits") to emphasize that every aspect of the Spirit's character should be evident in our lives. Some aspects are more evident than others in our lives, but all of them should be present to some degree.

A good resource on the various aspects of the fruit of the Spirit is Stephen Winward, *The Fruit of the Spirit* (Grand Rapids, Mich.: Eerdmans, 1984). Those who want to pursue an in-depth study of this area should see Hazel Offner's study guide the *Fruit of the Spirit* in the LifeBuilder Bible Study series.

Question 8. The sinful nature was crucified in the sense that we no longer have to live under its domination or control. We as Christians can choose to be obedient to the Spirit or to submit again to the old master's authority. When we submit to the flesh, we sin; when we submit to the Spirit, we grow in godliness.

Study 11. The Spirit Influences. Ephesians 5:15-21.

Purpose: To bring our lives into joyful submission to the Spirit of God.

Introduction: Some in your group may object to the idea of being "controlled" by the Holy Spirit. The fact is (as we have seen in studies 8 and 10): Everyone is controlled by something! Those who think they are in control of their own lives are in reality controlled by their sinful nature. It is only when we submit to the Spirit's influence that we experience genuine self-control (see Galatians 5:22-23).

Question 3. This is one of several places in the New Testament where a writer tells us explicitly what "the Lord's will" is. Only a foolish person would ignore Paul's instructions.

Question 4. The point of this question is not to generate a lengthy discussion on a Christian's use (or nonuse) of alcohol! Paul's concern is the *misuse* of anything that takes away our ability to submit to the Spirit of God. "Addiction" in any garb is not within the realm of God's will for any Christian.

Question 5. The phrase "to be filled" was often used in the New Testament to refer to control. (See, for example, John 16:6 and Acts 5:3, 17.) We are not to become so drunk that we are under alcohol's influence, but we are to be filled (controlled, influenced) by the Spirit.

Question 7. A Spirit-controlled person will display the fruit of the Spirit in every situation (see Galatians 5:22-23). Another way to explain it is to say that in Jesus we see a perfectly Spirit-filled person. So, when we are Spirit-filled, we will act like Jesus would act if he faced the situations, people, and problems we face.

Question 8. Several requirements can be gleaned from these verses. The person who desires to be filled with the Spirit should be walking in wisdom (v. 15) and obedience (v. 17) to the Lord. Since Paul *commands* us to be filled with the Spirit, it is obviously a matter of choice and responsibility on our part to submit willingly to the Spirit's direction and control in our lives.

Question 12. The filling of the Spirit is a matter of obedience, not necessarily a matter of emotion. We may not "feel" the Spirit's filling, but if we are walking in obedience to God's Word and are yielding ourselves to the Spirit, we can be confident that we are filled with the Spirit.

Study 12. The Spirit Unifies. Ephesians 4:1-16.

Purpose: To show the unity of purpose and goal that results from the Spirit's presence in the lives of believers.

Question 5. You may want to explore this issue on a deeper level by asking, "What happens to unity if we simply take a casual approach to it rather than pursue it with diligence?" Unity in a fellowship group or church does not just "happen." It is produced by the Spirit, but we are responsible to nurture it.

Question 6. Keep in mind that Paul is emphasizing these points of unity among those who acknowledge Jesus Christ as Savior and Lord. His points do not extend beyond the realm of genuine believers in Christ.

Question 7. The New Testament "apostles" and "prophets" were used by God to produce the Scriptures upon which we build our faith (see Ephesians 2:20). Contemporary parallels may be missionaries who are sent to preach Christ as the apostles were. Modern-day prophets may be seen in those men and women who speak with authority to our culture and to our nation to call us back to godly obedience. "Evangelists" go to those who have not heard the gospel. "Pastors and teachers" function primarily within the church to build up and strengthen believers. Paul's point is that these gifted individuals are responsible to prepare God's people for ministry. They are not to do the ministry for God's people.

Question 9. Just like spiritual gifts, our works of ministry are to build up the body of Christ in some way. The goal of ministry is to bring people to maturity in Christ.

Douglas Connelly is pastor of Cross Church. Doug and his wife, Karen, live in Flushing, Michigan, with their three children, Kimberley, Kevin and Kyle. Doug is also the author of the LifeBuilder Bible Studies Daniel *and* John.